HIS NAME IS...

THE EMINEM STORY IN WORDS AND PICTURES

TEXT BY SCOTT GIGNEY AND MARTIN HARPER,
ADDITIONAL MATERIAL BY ROB JOHNSTONE AND JAMES TOMALIN.
SCRIPT READING BY SYLWIA LUBKOWSKA.
DESIGN BY JON STOREY AND DAVID BALFOUR.
EDITED BY BILLY DANCER.

PRINTED AND BOUND IN THE UK.

his name is...

the eminem story in words and pictures

www.chromedreams.co.uk

For every 100 rock or pop performers, labelled with one of those much over-used accolades such as 'a true genius' or 'one of the greats', if even one of them stands up to scrutiny, it's a pretty good average. If such appraisals are being bandied around when the act is still considered a fairly 'new kid on the block', then you can bet your life the perpetrator's trying to sell you something.

But once in a while our cynicism is side-stepped as we sit up and listen a little closer. Perhaps there *is* something there. Something a little different. We can't quite put our fingers on it just yet, but we are prepared to keep our minds open a little longer to explore the possibilities.

In almost 50 years of pop culture there have certainly been a number of artists who have fallen into one of the above categories, but it normally takes many years before we can use such labels with confidence. Many contenders have fallen at the last hurdle and are remembered as being merely average. Others of course go the distance and are the true superstars of our age.

And so it is with Marshall Mathers III. Known to music fans the world over as Eminem, things are looking good for this young upstart. Although his music is set strictly in the genre known as hip-hop or rap, he's already reaching a far wider audience than would traditionally listen to that style. His subject matter has been regularly criticised for being violent, sexist or homophobic [although often, those normally most ready to point the finger for such offences, are staying conspicuously silent on this occasion]. But the general feeling seems to exist that there's a lot more to his message than anger and hatred.

Of course it goes without saying that Eminem's rap lyrics do contain a lot of pent-up anger, and in many cases understandably so when considering the background of abuse he suffered during his formative years. But so does the material of many other writers and performers, most of whom haven't achieved anything like the kind of popularity that Eminem has.

Eminem's songs and performances seem to be not only a release for his own feelings, but to work additionally as some kind of catharsis for those who watch and listen. Perhaps this provides a far healthier way of dealing with negative emotions than allowing them to build up inside and ultimately be directed at an innocent party. Many popular therapies today work by releasing the body's stored emotions, in a controlled environment, through shouting, screaming and hitting inanimate objects [in place of 'the real thing']. This isn't a new argument and is often put forward in defence of violent films, but it has a certain logic.

On the other hand perhaps, as so often happens, Andy Warhol's metaphorical 15 minutes of fame have been spread over 3 albums and this time next year a new hero emerges. Maybe just the ability to rhyme a few words and stick a catchy break in the middle is all that sells this guy's records. Vanilla Ice anyone?

To try and analyse a performer's popularity is, in many ways, futile. Ask 100 fans why they like a certain artist and you're sure to get 100 different replies. But futile as it may be, it's nevertheless a favourite waste of time for many of us. One thing's for certain, talent alone is no guarantee of commercial success, today's most accurate barometer of mass adulation. A measure of that is imperative of course, but many other ingredients must be present. Huge personal drive and ambition should coexist with bags of energy, and in modern times, the ability to shock. This last point is one of Eminem's trump cards. He's found a way to once again bring an element of danger to popular music that seems to of been missing for many years. Like Elvis Presley, The Rolling Stones, The Sex Pistols and The Beastie Boys before him, he's paralleled that ability with some fantastic material and unforgettable performances, to create a package that has moved a generation.

Eminem's shock tactics have largely been concerned with turning away from the politically correct attitudes present in a lot of the pop music produced over the last twenty years. But although this may be a new angle, the ultimate result remains the same as always: to annoy, anger and outrage one's elders. Presley did it by wiggling his hips, The New York Dolls by wearing communist regalia. The secret is to come out against anything your folks thought was right and proper. But still the reasons behind the music industry's biggest success story for ages, are unclear. There must have been other performers who had all the attributes listed above, yet they often went from being 'wannabes' to 'never weres' without creating a stir. Situations where the whole becomes less than the sum of its parts. Maybe, to paraphrase a current magazine advertisement, it's just that we're all 5 % Slim Shady. Perhaps the 'E' factor was missing.

This book however, offers no conclusions. We've attempted to inform and to stimulate thought and debate. We come to analyse, to reveal and to catalogue, but not to criticise or applaud. We don't attempt to alter anyone's personal views on the subject. Any answers are really just that. If this is the reader's aim, we hope we can be of some assistance.

Let's take a look at the evidence.

The Editor

MTV
MUSIC TELEVISION
video_music_awards
ma.oo
sic_awards
MUSIC TELEVISION
vards
ma.oo
_music_award

Halfway through the last decade of the 20th century, American music didn't seem to be in the healthiest of states. Grunge, the style which set the standard for rock in the early 1990's, had now been long extinguished by its own repetitive mediocrity, as the new bands of the day churned out sickeningly derivative music based on the structured blueprint of Nirvana, Soundgarden, Alice in Chains and Pearl Jam, without adding anything new or even barely interesting to this established formula. The Billboard and U.K. music charts were awash with a never-ending stream of awful pop ditties that numbed the listener's brain until all he could hear was the constant beat of the electronic bass drum. In addition to this atrocity, we also had inflicted upon us the continuous, pointless meanderings of countless girl and boy bands, sadly devoid of any semblance of musical talent and sporting the kind of saccharine lyrics that would make a hormonal teenager blush.

Heavy Metal was also in an extreme state of flux, with the whole scene feeling a collective disappointment due to the overall dullness of recent releases from the genre's main players and the somewhat worrying, different musical direction that the previously mighty Metallica had taken on their new record. Things were bleak and average and it didn't look like matters were going to get any brighter in the near future. But bad as these things were, nothing could compare to the trouble that rap and hip-hop were in at this time.

But while popular dance music has always been inane and brainless, almost by definition, and in truth there have always been girl and boy-based bands of widely varying degrees of talent, rap and hip-hop had previously always been 'hardcore'. The music and lyrics have normally been likened to modern day urban hymns, with the rappers standing up, standing out and acting as the 'spoke persons' for their generation, for the poor and disaffected youth of America. But now, for better or for worse, a new breed of rappers were appearing. Only this lot no longer wanted to be known as rappers, they wanted to be known as hip-hop *artists*. Their beats were weak and their lyrics were laughably pedestrian and uninspiring. Rap had been diluted so as to make it almost unrecognisable from its original form. The unthinkable had happened: hip-hop had gone pop.

It was fast becoming a desperately sad state of affairs. While the respected rappers of old continued in their own unique and inimitable styles, they just weren't doing enough business or selling enough records outside of their traditional circles to keep up with the young Turks who were clogging up the charts with their hip-pop. This caused many of the old school to call it a day and retire gracefully, deeply saddened by the genre's cruel demise. Where could rap go from here? How could hip-hop redeem itself? These were the questions that plagued the minds of every hardcore rapper and rap fan the world over.

Of course the rebirth started slowly and quietly. These things always do. People were rapping freestyle at small venues and tapes were being traded by a network of fans, a movement not seen since the days of the San Francisco Bay area 'thrash-metal' scene of the mid 80's, but an activity now made a whole lot easier by the use of the Internet. The ultimate irony in all this was that the bland and inoffensive pop music that the likes of Will Smith had been putting out as rap, had actually forced hip-hop

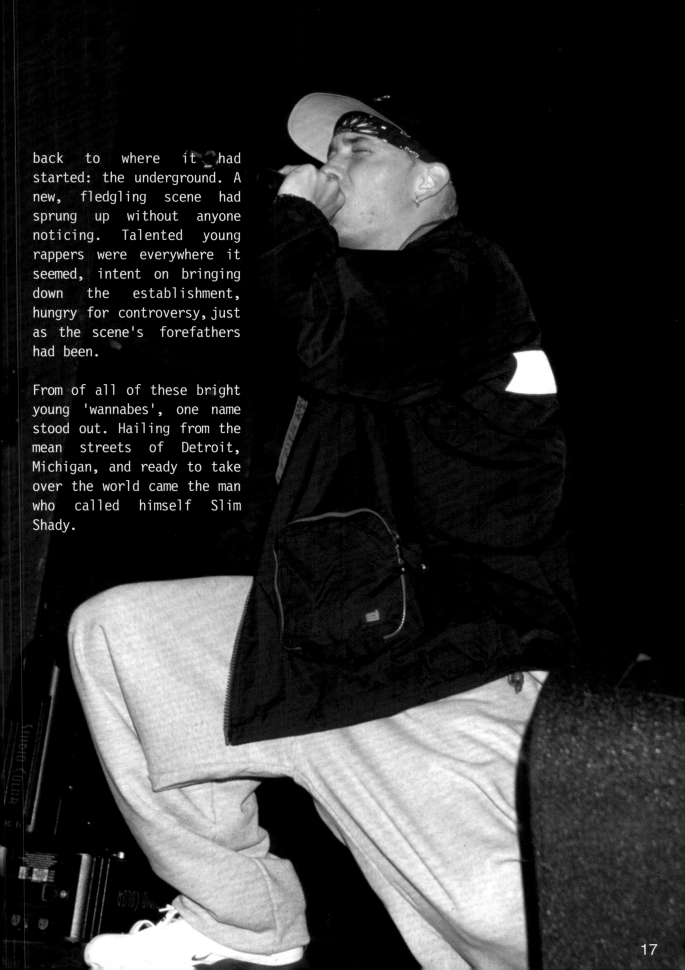

back to where it had
started: the underground. A
new, fledgling scene had
sprung up without anyone
noticing. Talented young
rappers were everywhere it
seemed, intent on bringing
down the establishment,
hungry for controversy, just
as the scene's forefathers
had been.

From of all of these bright
young 'wannabes', one name
stood out. Hailing from the
mean streets of Detroit,
Michigan, and ready to take
over the world came the man
who called himself Slim
Shady.

The remarkable tale of Eminem began in a rather unremarkable fashion. It all started in Kansas City, Missouri, in the year 1970 with Debbie Nelson, a pretty 15-year-old girl who was the singer for a popular local covers band, Daddy Warbucks. As is often the case, she fell in love with one of her band mates, Marshall Mathers Junior, who was seven years her senior. As soon as she was of legal age, they got married. On the 17th of October 1972, Debbie gave birth to her first child, a son. He was named Marshall Bruce Mathers III, and Debbie was ecstatic. Unfortunately, her husband wasn't quite so happy and six months after the birth of his son, Marshall Mathers Junior headed off to California, walking out of their lives forever.

The young Marshall's upbringing was sadly far from idyllic. Those who knew her felt that Debbie was more than a little unstable. She'd have constant mood swings that just could not be predicted. One moment she would be affable, attentive and affectionate towards her son, the next she'd be sitting quietly in a corner on her own, withdrawn from the world. On occasion she could jump up in your face and scream blue murder. As time went on, Marshall's mother was suspected of suffering from a mental disorder called Munchausen Syndrome by Proxy. This condition is alleged to make a parent believe that his or her perfectly fit and healthy child is ill. The parent forces the child to undergo numerous and unnecessary medical treatments. With that thought in mind, it is perhaps for the best that, during his formative years, Marshall was often left with one relative or another while Debbie went off to do her own thing. As a result of this, Marshall became extremely close to his mother's little brother, Ronnie Polkinghorn. To the young Marshall, Ronnie was more than his uncle or just another one of these distant relations, he was like his own brother and his best friend, which made what happened next all the harder for both the boys to handle.

In 1980, when Marshall had reached eight years of age, Debbie took her son and relocated from Missouri to Warren in East Detroit, Michigan. Marshall was devastated. He missed Ronnie terribly and became visibly withdrawn. This upset Debbie, as Marshall had always been such a happy child. But the move to Detroit wasn't the only problem playing on Marshall's young mind. Unbeknown to Debbie, every time he left the house he was terrorised by the neighbourhood bullies. He was constantly hunted down and beaten because he was small and couldn't defend himself. And because he was white. The problems that Marshall had to face at home were nothing compared to the unmitigated torment that he was forced to endure at school.

Every day proved to be a new chapter of pain for Marshall as he was put through a gamut of taunts and physical abuse at every break period, every lunch time and on every walk home. The bullying that Marshall suffered was far more than petty name-calling; it was vicious. But more disturbing was the fact that the bullies were methodical and deliberate in the way they tormented him. They did everything they could to ensure that this kid lived in terror from the first bell of the school day to the closing of the gates. The abuse came to a tragic head when Marshall entered the fourth-grade. It was during this period that he was terrorised virtually every day by one older pupil who was, needless to say, a much-feared bully. The beatings that this particular individual meted out were more violent than anything that Marshall had had to deal with in the past instances of abuse he'd suffered. The thug would beat him anywhere and everywhere, be it in the toilet, the cloakroom or even mere feet from the poor guy's front door. Unfortunately things were going from bad to worse and in the winter of 1983 life became simply unbearable for Marshall. He was faking illness in an attempt to stay away from the torment he was suffering at school. One day, during recess, the bully cornered Marshall in the playground and proceeded to hand out the most harrowing and violent attack that the kid had ever endured. As the battered youngster collapsed unconscious on the floor, the bully carried on kicking him in the head. This continued until he was pulled off by a teacher, who somehow hadn't realised what was happening until that moment. Although disorientated and confused, the dazed Marshall was sent home from school but started bleeding from his ears and was rushed to hospital with a cerebral haemorrhage, spending the next ten days in a coma. The swelling on his brain was so severe that the doctors admitted to Debbie that he may not of pulled through. Eventually, when he woke up he seemed unscarred both in body and mind, but he was now harbouring a hatred that would drive him on to success in later years.

After Marshall's close brush with death, Debbie decided that they couldn't stay in Detroit any longer and in the summer of 1984 they moved back home to Kansas City and back to Ronnie. The two boys were inseparable once again and spent all of their free time together. Marshall really looked up to his uncle, he was in awe of him and thought of him as a real bad-ass, although Ronnie was never anything less than a stand-up guy whenever he and Marshall were together. Being as enamoured as he was with him, it was little wonder that Marshall started to take an interest in Ronnie's hobbies and it turned out that he was a big fan of rap music. A talented rapper himself, he was quite happy to "beat box" and make amateur rap tapes for Marshall who loved them and listened to them constantly. But his real wake-up call came when, at the age of eleven, Ronnie played him a song called 'Reckless' by a Los Angeles rapper named Ice-T. It was that precise moment that he began to understand exactly what rap and hip-hop were all about.

3. the hip-hop genesis

From the early delta blues of the American South, to Chuck Berry in the 1950's, the Motown scene in the 60's and Jimi Hendrix in the 70's, black Americans have reflected their cultural heritage through rhythms in their music. In 1979, a frenetic fusion of disco and beat poetry hit the charts. 'Rapper's Delight' by the Sugarhill Gang became the first ever rap hit single. A new age in music had dawned.

The tunes produced by the original innovators of rap such as Grandmaster Flash and the Furious Five, Kurtis Blow and Dougie Fresh and the Get Fresh Crew became the clarion call for the disaffected, black youth of America. Though nowadays one may regard their music as old-school and minimalist, you still cannot deny or underestimate the impact that they subsequently had on the whole music scene. Hot on the heels of these rappers came further artists such as Run DMC from the Def Jam record label, and later the first white rap band to find success, The Beastie Boys. These acts regularly incorporated funk, disco and corrosive heavy-metal guitar samples into their hip-hop blue-print. This helped the artists to achieve an extremely aggressive impact, especially evident on the Beastie's 1986 album *License to Ill*, which featured the frantic guitar soloing of Kerry King from speed metal kings Slayer on the now legendary track, 'No Sleep 'Til Brooklyn'. *License to Ill* went on to become the first ever rap album to reach number one in the Billboard charts. Hip-hop was well and truly up and running.

Between the mid-1980's and the early 1990's, New York city was the home of hip-hop. LL Cool J, Rakim, Eric B, De La Soul, Salt 'n' Pepa, Public Enemy, a Tribe Called Quest and Queen Latifah were the prime of the hugely successful rap acts that kept the scene moving. But as the 90's took off, a new breed of rappers emerged on the West Coast of America. Since the mid-80's, Ice-T had been virtually the sole West Coast artist getting any East Coast respect or airplay, but now his young protégés were about to grab the mic and step up to bat against the New York crew. This was the advent of gangsta-rap.

Gangsta-rap emerged as a harsh, violent hip-hop sub-genre. Bands like NWA, Cypress Hill, Snoop Doggy Dogg, Boo Ya Tribe and of course, Ice-T himself, were the main exponents of West Coast gangsta-rap. But the East Coast took note and in very little time began to catch them up. Notorious B.I.G., Nas, The Wu-Tang Clan and the Gravediggaz all went to play for the East. A feud erupted and blood was shed. The gangstas of hip-hop were being slain just the same as the 'brothers' in Compton, South Central, Harlem, Brooklyn or the Bronx. Snoop went to court on murder charges and Tupac Shakur and Notorious B.I.G. were murdered in drive-by shootings. Gangsta-rap was falling apart at the seams with only Dr. Dre, Ice-T and Ice Cube as the still domi-nant forces in the hip-hop world. Puff Daddy, Jay-Z and Nas had watered hip-hop down in an attempt to make it more palatable for the masses, and hard-core hip-hop was in a bad way. Thankfully, there were artists waiting in the wings, ready to inject some blood and thunder back into the scene.

4. the mis-education of marshall mathers

Upon his return to Missouri, the time Marshall now spent with his uncle Ronnie was the happiest of his life up to that point. His mother was in a more stable condition, which was good news for the young Marshall. In 1986 she even had another child, Eminem's half-brother Nathan. But twelve months later, after three years of an almost blissful existence, Debbie packed up house and once again moved, with Marshall and Nathan in-tow, back to Detroit. This time the move was a permanent one and he was left heartbroken by his second separation from Ronnie. Once in Detroit however, he began to recover quickly from this depression. Although over the previous three years he had become a hardcore rap fan, Marshall had never felt comfortable with the idea of rapping in Ronnie's presence. He felt incredibly self-conscious, not least because Ronnie was an extremely talented rapper who really had a knack for rhyming. But now Marshall turned the move back to Detroit into something really positive. He began to rap seriously, making up beat tapes and rhyming to them. Much to his own surprise, he was pretty good. His years of watching Ronnie like a hawk were starting to pay dividends.

At the age of 14, Marshall began actively writing lyrics for his raps. He started utilising the beat-box techniques that Ronnie had imparted to him to record his own hip-hop tracks. As he continued practising, his rapping became faster and more lyrically focused. He was really getting a feel for the vocal rhythm patterns that all rappers must have. It was at this point that Marshall took on his own rap alias, Eminem. The name came simply from his initials, M and M. He liked the new name as it was still close to his own, though expressed in a completely different way. Following the adoption of his alternative moniker, Eminem started to make waves at the high school at which he had enrolled. Much to his delight, it turned out that "battle rapping" was a popular playground pastime. It involved going head to head with another rapper and trading off rhymes. The first to lose the flow or get tongue-tied lost the battle, but being in Detroit that wasn't all they lost. As kids, these young rappers couldn't legally bet anywhere, so they took to gambling on the hip-hop face-offs. Since he was vastly superior to the majority of his peers, Eminem won consistently, making a nice bit of money for himself in the process. Actually, he won so often that after a while no one could be persuaded to face him. They knew that defeat would be inevitable. Eminem earned a great deal of respect in the playground and for the first time he truly realised that being a rapper was definitely going to be a viable option for him, as long as he continued to practice and to hone his rhyming skills. This was also the first time in his life that Marshall had been shown any respect.

His confidence serged and, at 15 years of age, Eminem met the girl who would become his high school sweetheart, and eventually his wife, Kimberley Scott. It was also at this time that he formed his first rap group with school friends, under the banner of Bassmint Productions. Although he nominally attended Lincoln Junior High, over the following two years he skipped school constantly. Like most kids he found it a total drag, especially as he felt that his time could be better spent rapping. After all, he was going to become a famous rapper, so what the hell should he care about chemistry, high school pep rallies or algebra? Eminem continued skipping classes up until the age of 17 when he dropped out altogether after failing the ninth-grade for the third time. He was intent on pursuing his dream and sent out tapes of his rapping, which led to an invitation to perform regularly on the open mic nights at a local radio station. He was told that he was pretty good… for a white guy! But this back-handed complement only served to fuel Eminem's fire, making him more intent on striving toward the successful realisation of his ambition.

In the summer of 1992, Ronnie came to stay with Eminem in Detroit. Eminem was naturally ecstatic to have his uncle around once more and spent all his time in Ronnie's company. He realised that he had come a long way since moving from Missouri to Michigan and finally felt comfortable telling Ronnie about his dreams of being a rap star. Ronnie's response turned out to be a whole lot less positive than Eminem had expected. He told his nephew that he had given up rapping for good and that Eminem's dreams were just that, dreams. His words left Eminem deflated, but also instilled in him a determination to never lose his hope, like Ronnie obviously had.

Eminem was desperate for a break and his prayers were answered in the winter of '92, when he was offered the opportunity to perform onstage at the Saturday night freestyle contests that were held at the Hip-Hop Shop on Detroit's West Mile. His excitement at the prospect was total, but the bubble burst as he took to the stage. The crowd started booing the rapper and continued to do so throughout the duration of his set. They steadfastly refused to give him a chance, but while they may have upset him that night, they also gave him the will and determination to return. The club's owner, however, had been impressed by Eminem's resilience in the face of such open hostility, and offered him the chance to come back. He agreed immediately and over the course of the following year kept doggedly plugging away, entering the rap competitions held at the club every weekend. The more appearances he put in, the more he seemed to win the crowd over. He was finally gaining the respect he deserved and, before too long, he was winning virtually every week. Based on his club performances, he was offered the chance to rap on WHYT, the biggest hip-hop radio station in the city. This was a doubly exciting proposition, as numerous other rappers had gained record deals after their appearances on the show. Eminem was now totally focused and ready to grasp the opportunity. But all his hard work came crashing down around him like a house of cards when tragedy came calling for Marshall Mathers.

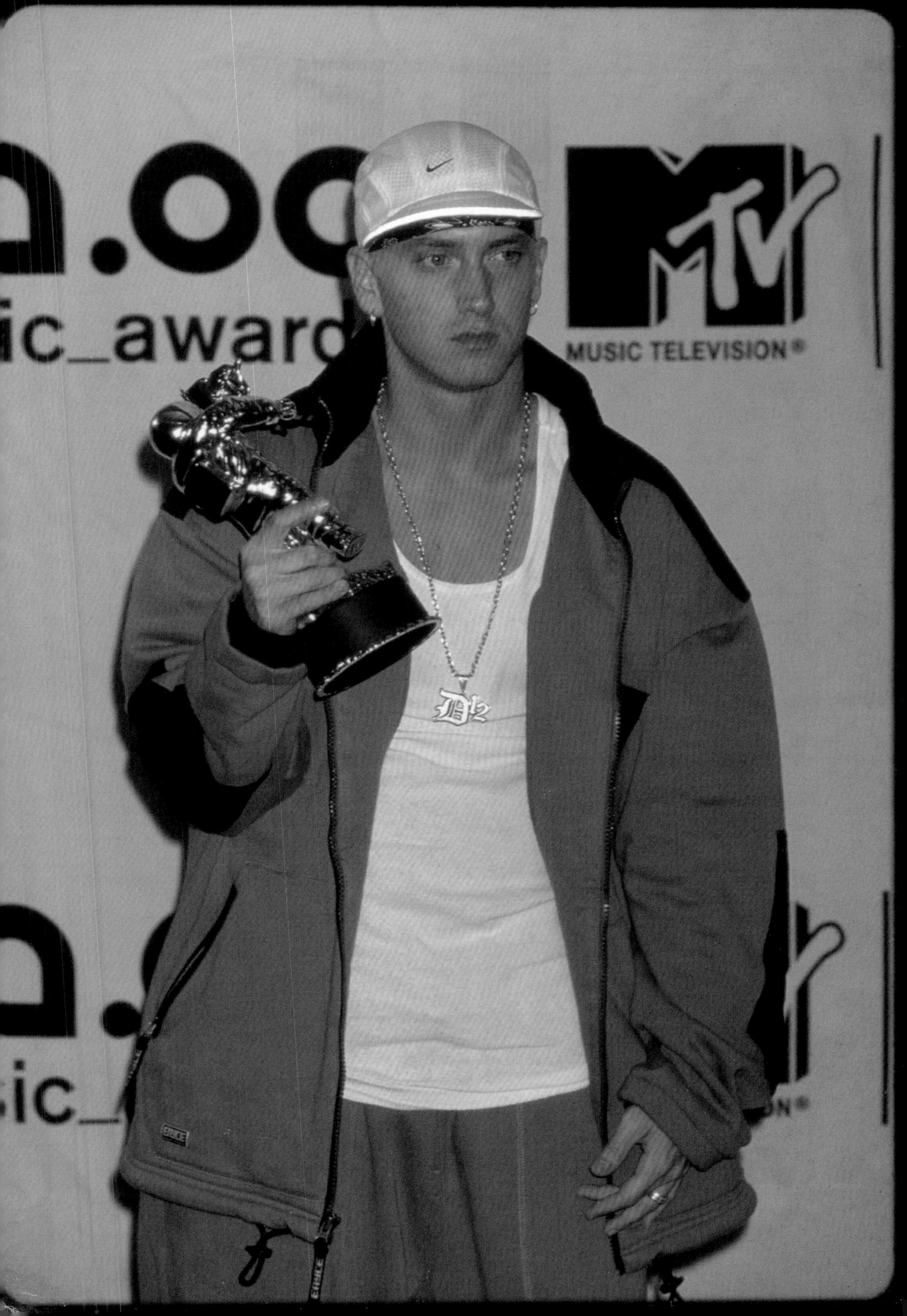
ic_award
MTV
MUSIC TELEVISION®
D12

S. darkness and illumination

On the 13th of December 1993, Eminem was hanging out at a friend's house, when he received a phone call from his mother. As he took the phone from his friend, he could hear his mother crying on the other end of the line. When he asked her what was wrong, she could only manage to reply with a fresh volley of sobs. Eventually he was able to calm her down enough in order that she could speak. But he soon wished he hadn't. Debbie blurted out the two most heartbreaking words that Eminem could imagine: "Ronnie's dead". The icy tentacle of fear squeezed Eminem's heart as he ran home to console his mother, yet still he couldn't believe it was true and was in need of consolation himself. How could Ronnie be dead?

When he got home the horror was confirmed, Ronnie was indeed dead, he had killed himself. The shock that Eminem felt was absolute. While his mother seemed content to cry herself to sleep, he just could not stop thinking about what had happened. What could have depressed his uncle to such an extent that he'd take his own life rather than seek help? Eminem blamed himself. His rationale was that if Ronnie had called him first and talked things over, then he wouldn't have done what he did. It was a warped logic that only served to make the grieving Eminem feel even more sorry for himself. He obviously wasn't at fault in any way, shape or form for the tragedy, but the desire to rationalise Ronnie's death led to a horrible feeling of guilt that weighed heavily on his shoulders.

Eventually, his guilt gave way to emptiness and deep, deep depression. He was inconsolable, and nothing that his mother nor his girlfriend Kim said could pull him out of the hole he had dug for himself. For the first time since he was 14, Eminem stopped writing and rapping. He spent all his days in his room listening to Ronnie's rap tapes, playing them over and over again. It was almost as if he believed that Ronnie would come back if he heard his voice rapping out a constant mantra. The depression continued for over a year and in all that time he didn't pick up his writing pen once. But on the 15th of March 1995, he received a piece of news that was to be his remedy. Kim sat him down and told him that she was pregnant, and that he was going to be a father!

Kim gave birth to a bouncing baby girl on Christmas Day 1995. Eminem's happiness knew no bounds and he and Kim decided jointly to call their daughter Hailie Jade. This pivotal event proved to be a real eye-opener for Eminem, and he made the decision to pull himself up by his boot laces and start living life again. He was determined to be a good father to Hailie and provide for her in all the ways that his own father had failed to for him. Eminem came to realise that all he really wanted to do for a living was his music and that it was about time he got back to work. Within a few months Eminem returned to rap with a renewed determination and fresh inspiration.

He teamed up with friend DJ Buttafingaz to create the duo Soul Intent, recording what was to be his first commercially released tracks on the eponymous EP *Soul Intent*. Through his hard work it didn't take too long for him to create a huge buzz around himself on the underground scene.

He came to the attention of a small company called FBT Productions. FBT, or the Funky Bass Team, consisted of a pair of Detroit hip-hop producers called Marky and Jeff Bass. They had heard Eminem rapping on the WHYT late-night radio show in Detroit and were so impressed that they approached him, offering the chance to record a debut album. It was an offer that was too good to refuse for the young rapper. As he came to make the record, Eminem was advised to pen "radio friendly" songs. He duly obliged and produced a series of largely uplifting compositions written about his daughter and his contented family life. Eminem's debut album *Infinite* was released in the autumn of 1996. Unfortunately, it attracted no airplay at all and achieved virtually no sales. In fact, so poor was the response that Eminem was forced to sell copies on the street out of the trunk of his car. Moreover, the local hip-hop community roundly criticised the recording, as they felt that he sounded too much like the more established rappers Nas and Jay-Z. Eminem later played down his performance on the album saying that it was more like a demo than a complete work. He now prefers to think of *Infinite* as being representative of a time when he was finding his voice, a time when he was growing as an artist rather than charting the definitive moment when he actually arrived. Although *Infinite* did show signs of what Eminem was capable of, and certainly gave him valuable recording experience, the lack of sales made it look like an unmitigated disaster and the FBT team began to worry that they may never see a return on their investment.

All this left Eminem in complete creative limbo, but just as it looked as though things could get no worse, they did just that. Eminem, Kim and Hailie were evicted from their apartment. Because of money troubles, he couldn't afford to pay the rent or even buy diapers for his daughter. Although he was subsidising his music-making by working part-time as a chef at Gilbert's Lodge, a restaurant in St Clair Shores, he was barely making ends meet. Due to all the stress at this point, Kim left Eminem and took Hailie with her. She moved back home with her parents and Eminem was denied access to his daughter, not even being allowed to go into the house to see her. These events sent Eminem down into another spiral of depression, and in December 1996 history repeated itself when Eminem made a serious suicide attempt of his own by overdosing on prescription sleeping pills. He survived the overdose, but as he recovered, he felt unbridled rage coursing through his veins. Pouring all his fury and frustration back into his rapping, Slim Shady was born.

Slim Shady was Eminem's evil alter ego and a plain statement of intent, the premise being that everyone has a dark side to their personality. He had first come up with the name in January 1997, when his then group collaborators D12

The man who is known throughout the world as Dr. Dre was born plain old Andre Young, on the 18th of February 1965 in South Central Los Angeles. He was an exceptional child who seemed to be able to turn his hand to anything, especially anything musical. In the guise of Dr. Dre, he would eventually go on to become one of the originators of the West Coast gangsta-rap movement, and amongst *the* most celebrated producers in hip-hop history.

Dre always knew what he wanted to do, and embarked upon a musical career at an early age. His first job was as a DJ at a Los Angeles dance club called Eve After Dark. It was there that Dre first experimented with the splicing together of such artists as different in style as Martha and the Vandellas and George Clinton. The club also had a small back-room studio where Dre and his future NWA (Niggaz With Attitude) collaborator Yella would record demo tapes. These sessions taught Dre many different turn-table techniques that he would eventually come to perfect in his future musical projects. The formation of the petrol bomb explosion that was NWA, sent shockwaves through Middle America. With songs like 'Straight Outta Compton' and 'Fuck Tha Police', NWA struck fear into the hearts of every racist cop and politician in the land. Such was the furore they caused that the Federal Bureau of Investigation actually went to the lengths of researching the history of all the individual group members, compiling an extensive dossier on them. The kids of America wholeheartedly embraced NWA. Like the punk scene of the late 70's, hip-hop was now all about rebelling against authority. NWA had become *the* premier gangsta-rap band. However, the group didn't last and before long NWA collapsed under a heap of inter-band wrangling, resulting in Ice Cube, Eazy E and Dr. Dre all going solo. Whilst Ice Cube and Eazy E both proved to be extremely popular as solo acts, it was Dre that was to alter the face of hip-hop forever. After a few brushes with the law, that was.

Like many of the big names in rap, Dr. Dre never strayed far from controversy. In 1991 American television host Dee Barnes filed a multi-million dollar lawsuit against him for allegedly throwing her against the wall of a Hollywood night-club. Dre was also convicted of breaking the jaw of a record producer, resulting in him being placed under house arrest and being fitted with a tracking device. To top it all off, Dre was detained by police officers in a New Orleans hotel lobby after a scrap. But somehow, despite these unwanted distractions, Dre still managed to produce the most talked-about hip-hop record of the 1990's.

The release of Dre's seminal *The Chronic* in 1993 was greeted with mass hysteria. The album name came from the moniker given to a particularly strong brand of weed and, along with such luminaries as Cypress Hill, he confirmed once and for all that cannabis was the drug of choice for the modern gangsta rapper. The record's hectic beats, funky samples and vicious raps made *The Chronic* the biggest selling hip-hop disc of the year. In addition to this, it also gained Dr. Dre two Grammy awards, including one for Best Solo Rap Performance on the hit single, *Let Me Ride*. The album went on to spend eight months in the Billboard Top Ten.

Dre basked in the success for a while, although he had been in the hip-hop game long enough to know that complacency is a deadly sin. With this fact in mind, Dre poured all of his energy into a myriad of musical projects. His main interest was to produce records and he had a real talent for it. There was a buzz around Dre and everyone on the West Coast wanted him to arrange their records. He went on to produce for Eazy E, D.O.C. and Above The Law, but by far the most important rapper he worked with was Snoop Doggy Dogg. Snoop was a big name on the underground and had already rapped with Dre on the hit singles *Deep Cover* and *Nuthin' But A "G" Thang*, but still hadn't entered the upper echelons of West Coast gangsta rap. That changed when Snoop drafted in Dr. Dre to produce his debut album, *Doggy Style*, which was released on the same label Dre was signed to, Death Row Records. *Doggy Style* was a huge success and went on to sell millions. This, coupled with the success of *The Chronic* and the signing of one of rap's biggest new superstars, Tupac Shakur, turned Death Row into one of the most powerful record labels in America. But all was not well, and by 1996 Dr. Dre had grown sick and tired of internal politics at the label, and he left under a cloud in acrimonious circumstances. But, he was far from finished and swiftly set up a new label, aptly named Aftermath. Aftermath's first release was a various artists compilation which featured Dre's own Death Row baiting track, 'Been There Done That'.

Dre spent the next couple of years running his label. He signed the artists he wanted to sign and produced the records he wanted to produce. He was enjoying the fruits of his labour and taking things easy. That is, until he stumbled over a copy of *The Slim Shady EP*.

7. call me slim

After the success of *The Slim Shady LP*, Eminem could have been forgiven for thinking that everything would now be nice and easy. In June of 1999 he and Kim had gotten married and life was treating him well. That was until it was brought to his attention that his mother, Debbie Mathers-Briggs, was suing him for $10 million dollars for defamation of character. This came about as the result of interviews that Eminem had given on radio's nationally syndicated Howard Stern Show as well as in the magazines *Rap Pages*, *The Source* and *Rolling-Stone*, in which he made various references to his mother's drug taking and lack of parental skills. The lawsuit, which was filed on the 17th of September 1999 in Macomb County Court, Mount Clemens, Michigan, claimed that through the publication of these statements Eminem had caused her to suffer both physical and psychological injury. However, the lawsuit didn't really surprise Eminem, and he didn't take it too seriously. His defence rested on his insistence that everything he'd said was true (he knew his mother better than most).

And to balance things out, Eminem was then to receive some excellent news. Interscope Records, the parent company of Dr. Dre's Aftermath label, to which Eminem was signed, were prepared to offer him the opportunity to create and run *his* own record label. He would be given total control over which groups or artists he wanted to sign and could pretty much do what he wanted. Eminem readily took the chance and in September 1999 he formed Shady Records. Unfortunately, he couldn't spend too much time working on his new label just yet, as he was planning a new album of his own.

In early October, while his new album was in genesis, Eminem was involved in a widely reported incident during an interview on college radio station KALX 90.7 FM in Berkley, California. The presenter, Sister Tamu, had sat Eminem down before the show and gone over some ground rules with him. These included keeping the show clean and not straying too far in his freestyles in order that it didn't offend her Sunday-morning audience. The interview progressed well and even though Eminem was annoyed by several references she made to his being white, he managed to keep his cool. Things began to degenerate when a listener called up and asked him to show off his freestyling. He launched into a rap, but got carried away dropping in a reference to slapping a pregnant woman. This was too much for Tamu, who pulled him off the air, threw him out of the studio and then, complaining bitterly about his behaviour and promising never to have him back, cracked her copy of *The Slim Shady LP* in half live on air.

In early November 1999, Eminem entered the studio to record his follow-up to *The Slim Shady LP*. The new record proved to be just as dark and offensive as his previous one, but this time Eminem added the talents of his rap crew D12 to the mix. *The Marshall Mathers LP* was released in the US in May 2000 and proceeded to blow the success of *The Slim Shady LP* out of the water, by selling over two million copies in its first week of release. He was quick to capitalise on this success, and swiftly released the hit single *The Real Slim Shady*, in which, amongst others, he disses the hoards of now prevalent

Eminem imitators. The accompanying video, directed by Philip Atwell and Dr. Dre, is a quite hilarious look inside the head of the notorious Slim Shady. It even features cameo appearances from actress Kathy Griffin, Fred Durst from Limp Bizkit, Carston Haley of MTV and his old mucker, Kid Rock. The video was rapturously received, with the single selling by the truckload. His collaboration with Dr Dre *'Forgot About Dre'* also became a big hit. Things looked peachy for Eminem, but he was about to put it all in jeopardy.

10. will the real slim shady please stand up?

Feuds between hip-hop artists are a regular occurrence, and Eminem has proved no exception to this. One of the many groups that he has publicly spoken out against are the 'horrorcore' rap outfit The Insane Clown Posse. The ICP who, like Eminem, are white rappers from Detroit, started out as The Inner City Posse in the early 1990's, with two resident MCs, Shaggy 2 Dope (Joseph Ulster) and Violent J (Joseph Bruce). The Posse, who have also wrestled in the WWF and WCW, have attracted much media attention over their politically incorrect and vitriolic lyrics and have a reputation for their willingness to insult and outrage polite society. Allying themselves with the heavy metal community rather than the hip-hop world, one target of their unrestrained abuse was the wave of white rappers that were emerging, in particular Eminem and his friend Kid Rock.

Their rivalry stems back to 1995, when both Eminem and ICP were trying to make a name for themselves in and around Detroit. Eminem had been booked to play during an upcoming party in the city at St. Andrew's Hall and attempted to promote the event by handing out flyers in the area. Allegedly, these also stated that the Insane Clown Posse would be performing at the same event. They were incensed when they saw a copy of his flyer and thought that Eminem had been trying to capitalise on their name in order to get extra numbers to attend his gigs. ICP decided not to do anything about it at the time but the resentment has simmered away ever since, finding vocal expression on tracks such as 'Nuttin But A Bitch Thang' and 'Slim Anus'.

The bleached-blonde rapper himself lost no time in fighting back, including a personal message to the Posse on *The Marshall Mathers LP*. On the title track *Marshall Mathers*, Eminem suggests that Violent J and Shaggy 2 Dope were closet homosexuals, calling them 'Faggot 2 Dope' and 'Silent Gay' and criticising them, amongst other things, for claiming Detroit as their city when they lived twenty miles away. He then continues to diss them in the skit 'Ken Kaniff', where he lyrically depicts (in graphic terms) an encounter between them and a male prostitute.

This whole affair came to a head on the afternoon of the 3rd of June 2000 when Eminem encountered one of the Posse's entourage outside a car audio store in Royal Oak, Michigan. The employee, Douglas Dail, began arguing with Eminem almost immediately, although the actual cause of the dispute remains unclear. The pair continued to fight for several minutes, becoming more and more aggressive, until Eminem allegedly drew a 9mm semi-automatic Smith & Wesson pistol from an ankle holster and began to wave it in Dail's face. Unsurprisingly, Dail backed down quickly. Eminem's and Dail's wives had also begun shouting, but they stopped as soon as they saw the gun. The dispute ended shortly afterwards, with Dail and his wife returning to their car and leaving the scene.

Oddly enough, it was several hours before the incident was reported to the police. Eminem was duly arrested, being charged with brandishing a firearm and possession of a concealed weapon. The county prosecutor conceeded that Eminem had not actually pointed the gun at Dail, but he had used it in a threatening manner. He also revealed that Douglas Dail had withdrawn his earlier statement to the police, and was now refusing to co-operate with the investigation. No explanation for this strange behaviour was given, but it could suggest that Dail was the man chiefly responsible for initiating the fight.

Eminem has also had an ongoing feud with New York Rapper Cage since the release of the *The Slim Shady EP* in 1998. After hearing this record, Cage declared vocally in the media that Eminem had ripped-off his style. He then crystallised this complaint in the song 'Four Letter Word' and went on to diss Eminem further in tracks such as 'And So Kiddies', where he criticises Eminem's constant airplay on MTV. Eminem's retorts include the song 'Role Model' on *The Slim Shady LP*, where he states that he bought a tape by Cage but recorded over it, and the unreleased track 'Drastic Measures' where he mocks Cage by claiming that he intends to pick his sister up. Despite this very prolific feud, it is generally considered that Cage is only out to court controversy with the high-profile Eminem so that he can gain exposure for his own career.

Eminem's war of words with former House Of Pain rapper Everlast is yet another feud that refuses to go away. Everlast, or to give him his real name Whitey Ford, started the war by criticising Eminem during a guest appearance on a remixed version of the Dilated People's track 'Ear Drum Pop'. Eminem retorted with the song 'I Remember', which can be found on the B-Side of the D12 release *Shit On You*. On this track Eminem lampoons Everlast's switch from MC rapping to the more song-orientated style of his recent solo albums and states that he wished Everlast's 1998 heart-attack had killed him. Everlast has promised to release a reply to Eminem on a future record which he intends to be an underground release.

Amongst the scores of non-rappers who have incurred his wrath, Backstreet Boys, 'N Sync, Christina Aguilera and Britney Spears are near the top of the list. Indeed, after listening to the sexually explicit references to Christina on 'The Real Slim Shady', no one could overestimate the low esteem in which Eminem holds her. This whole beef came about due to her self-hosted 'What A Girl Wants' special on MTV. During the show she played Eminem's *My Name Is…* video but mentioned in passing that he was in fact married. At the time this was restricted information but thanks to Aguilera, now the whole world knew. She then proceeded to criticise what she believed was his promotion of domestic violence, coun-selling women everywhere to remove themselves from abusive relationships. This was all too much for Eminem who moved her swiftly up his hit list.

As a result of these numerous public spats, Eminem won the award for Most Entertaining Public Feud at the inaugural My VH-1 Music Awards on 30th November 2000. In order to avoid the somewhat dull nature of award ceremonies in general, VH-1 had decided to allow the viewers to agree on the categories that would be included, and the 'Feud Award' proved to be one of the most popular. Eminem was given the prize for his feud with 'Everyone', since he had spent the past year arguing with just about everyone he came into contact with.

In spite of all the heat generated by these public feuds, it was a private matter that left Eminem facing further gun-related charges. This time the incident involved his wife Kimberley. On the 4th of June 2000, Kim was spending the evening with friends at a local restaurant called the Hot Rocks Sports Bar and Café in Warren, Michigan. An establishment that she and Eminem regularly visited. Unfortunately, around midnight, Eminem himself appeared at the club with a friend following his suspicions that Kim was having an affair. Seeing Kimberley in an embrace with male friend John Guerra, he became enraged and flew at the pair, dragging his wife off and shouting at the man. Once again, Eminem drew a gun and began waving it at Guerra. The incident was over quickly, as Kimberley dragged her husband home. The café's security guard, however, called the police and notified them that a gun had been drawn. Shortly afterwards Eminem was arrested once again on a charge of assault with a deadly weapon and carrying a concealed weapon without a license. Guerra claimed that the rap star had hit him with the gun repeatedly, although Eminem denied this and pleaded not guilty. Kimberley maintained that there was no relationship between her and Guerra, and that the embrace was strictly platonic. Bail was set at $100,000, which Eminem's management team put forward, and the star was free again within hours.

Kimberley, however, was not so easily placated. She had been charged with breach of the peace for shouting abuse at the police when they came to arrest Eminem, but the whole situation had now become too much for her. The following morning she moved out of the family house in Sterling Heights, Michigan, taking Hailie Jade with her. Domestic disputes between Eminem and Kimberley were not unusual, although few of those closest to the couple sensed how serious the damage was until after this last incident. Kim had been unhappy with the relationship for some time, but had remained silent about the problems. She had been especially affected by one of the songs on *The Marshall Mathers LP*, 'Kim', as well as ''97 Bonnie and Clyde' from the previous album, both of which contained explicit references to murdering one's wife. The track named after her was particularly painful, since it detailed a scenario where a husband stabs his wife for sleeping with another man, something that Eminem had accused Kimberley of on occasions. Eventually, the pressures became too much and she collected her belongings and left home.

But Kimberley's mental state was more fragile than had been first suspected. Kim, and Eminem's half- brother Nate, had returned to the house in Sterling Heights after one of his shows on the 7th of July. She had slashed her wrists five times before she was found by Nate who called the para- medics. She was then taken to Mount Clemens General Hospital suffering from serious blood loss, where doctors patched up the self- inflicted wounds with over 150 stitches. Eminem was reported to be shocked by the news and did visit her in hospital before she was released, although both sides have steadfastly refused to comment on this painful matter.

The rapper withdrew from public life for a while, preferring to concentrate on his personal and legal prob- lems. His current album continued to sell well, fuelled by the extensive free publicity that seemed to cover Eminem's every move. Preparations were made to release 'The Way I Am' as the next single, accompanied by a surprisingly sedate video. The two guest stars on the film were Eminem's daughter Hailie Jade and shock-rock maestro Marilyn

11. can i kick it?

Unfortunately for Eminem, however, that wasn't the end of his current legal problems. His mother had offered him a settlement deal, which involved her dropping the defamation of character suit if he paid her two million dollars up-front. Offended by this blatant attempt to buy him out, he refused the offer. In return, his mother filed yet another defamation suit, this time with the civil courts (the first was in the criminal courts). This second suit claimed damages of one million dollars, on top of the ten million she was already seeking from her initial suit. Despite the astonishing sums of money involved, Eminem took this well, and delivered his deposition to the courts in a confident tone of voice. According to him, the lines from the single *My Name Is...*, claiming his mother used more dope than he did, referred to her intake of anti-depressants and tranquillisers during the rapper's childhood. He explained that his mother had been diagnosed with a number of mental health problems when she was younger and had been taking a sizeable quantity of medication. The lines in question did not refer, said Eminem, to marijuana, but to legally prescribed drugs.

Eminem's deposition was only one small part of the proceedings. Meanwhile, the rapper prepared to hit the road again, this time in the company of rap-rock outfit Limp Bizkit, as part of that band's 'Anger Management Tour'. The tour, which kicked off on the 19th of October 2000 in East Rutherford, New Jersey, was a mixture of rap and rock acts, including DMX and Papa Roach, although the spotlight was most firmly fixed on Eminem and the headliners, who had been friends since singer Fred Durst's appearance in *The Real Slim Shady* video. Eminem came onstage wearing a hockey mask and wielding a chainsaw, a tribute to some of his favourite horror movies. The rapper's recent troubles had clearly not dulled his edge, and the 'Anger Management' performances were widely agreed to be the finest of his career to date, fuelled by a passion and professionalism that had not always been present in his earlier shows.

Like the 'Up In Smoke Tour' a few months before, the 'Anger Management Tour' also became embroiled in controversy. Before it was due to cross the Canadian border for a performance in Toronto on the 26th of October, a local media-violence campaigner, Valerie Smith, made legal moves to prevent Eminem's entry into the country. She filed a criminal complaint with the Toronto Police hate crimes unit on the 4th of October arguing that his violent lyrics should be classified as hate propaganda under section 319 of the Canadian Criminal Code. This states that it is illegal to make statements that wilfully promote hatred against an 'identifiable group'. The day before the concert, Ontario Attorney General, Jim Flaherty, ruled in support of the ban as he believed that Eminem was likely to perform songs that advocated violence towards women. He therefore instructed immigration officials to stop

Despite this, when it came to the crunch on the following day, officials from the Citizenship and Immigration Authority determined that there were no legal grounds under which they could refuse him entry. It was argued that in the Canadian Criminal Code, an "identifiable group" only refers to color, race, religion or ethnic origin and not sex. As a result, Eminem was allowed in to the country and performed that night to a full-house at Toronto's Skydrome. Naturally, he started the concert with 'Kill You', one of the songs that had sparked off the attempt to ban him, and even dedicated 'The Way I Am' to Valerie Smith as a back-handed thank-you. Strangely, despite all the protests, no one present made a single complaint about the show. A week later though, almost exactly the same thing happened again when a group of ten University of Illinois students tried to force a similar ban before a concert at the Urbana-Champaign campus. Once more however, in the face of controversy, the tour was allowed to proceed with University officials finding no reason to keep it out.

At the end of September 2000, Eminem found himself at the centre of a Senate Commerce Committee hearing on violence in the American media. This came about as the result of a report by the Federal Trade Commission, which concluded that the entertainment industry was producing, and specifically marketing, material with adult content to American teenagers. Eminem in particular was singled out by Lynne Cheyne, wife of the then Republican vice-presidential candidate Dick Cheney, who criticised him in the strongest terms possible for writing lyrics which, in her opinion, promoted violence against women. She then laid into Seagram, the parent company of Eminem's label Interscope, connecting their release of artists such as Eminem and Marilyn Manson to recent high-school shootings like that at Columbine High School in Colorado.

In fact, no other artist even comes close to upsetting the moral gatekeepers of American culture to the same extent as Eminem. Depending on who he has riled, Eminem is variously accused of being misogynistic and homophobic, and has attracted a substantial amount of criticism for glorifying rape and violence. Amongst others, he has had run-ins with the Gay-Lesbian Alliance Against Defamation (GLAAD), who object to what they see as his negative attitude towards homosexuals. He has also been attacked by members of the National Organisation for Women, who hold that his outspoken lyrics go a long way towards developing and maintaining a climate in which violence against women is tolerated. They believe strongly that someone who has fantasies about murdering his wife shouldn't be celebrated and lauded as a media icon, and that awards from organisations like MTV simply give a rubber stamp to his opinions.

Although he acknowledges that his songs can be inherently shocking and outrageously controversial, Eminem is clear on this matter. He considers that his lyrics should not be taken literally or as representative of what he actually believes. To take the often quoted homophobia as an example, Eminem asserts very strongly in interviews that he is not homophobic. Although he says that he doesn't personally approve of the gay lifestyle, he doesn't have anything against homosexuals. As far as he is concerned, that is the business of those involved and their business alone. He claims he was surprised when he first heard that many were construing the use of the word 'faggot' in his lyrics to mean he was a gay-hater. He swears that he doesn't use this in the accepted sense to necessarily refer to gays, but as a general term for weak people. He is also keen to point out that he is on a one-man mission to push forward the boundaries of what is permissible in music. Indeed, it can be argued that you couldn't really expect him to consciously disturb the balance of normality without upsetting a few people along the way. Moreover, his music is always clearly labelled with an advisory sticker, stating that only eighteen-year-olds and over can purchase it, and Eminem and his production crew go to great lengths to produce 'clean' versions of his tracks that are toned down for general consumption on radio and TV. He claims that rather than blaming him, the censors should look more to the retailers and parents.

Eminem's next brush with authority was a little less serious. After finding his mailbox set on fire and countless 'M&M' packets thrown onto his front lawn, the latter presumably in good humour, the rapper decided to install an eight-foot fence around his property, with security cameras and a row of spikes across the top. But the local Residents' Association objected, saying it would make the neighbourhood look 'tacky'. However, as a compromise, given the specific nature of his problems, the Association allowed Eminem to build a shorter, six-foot fence around his $450,000 home.

The fourth single from *The Marshall Mathers LP* was released in November 2000. In a surprising move it was decided that the downbeat, atmospheric track 'Stan' would be the next release. In contrast to the earlier singles, it relied less upon Eminem's passion and anger, and more on his ability to construct a well-crafted lyric. 'Stan' was a typically dark offering, based around the story of an obsessive and unstable fan who takes his anger out on his pregnant girlfriend, after she voices concern about his growing obsession with the blonde rapper. The song features samples of British singer Dido, who expressed enthusiasm for the project, and was pleased to have her voice used on an Eminem single.

The video for the single attracted a good deal of controversy, as it depicted Stan attacking his girlfriend when she confronts him, over his secret horde of pictures of Eminem, and the letters he's written to his hero. Most music channels refused to play the video in its entirety until after nine p.m., although thankfully it was not banned outright. Eminem did though pick up a clutch of awards at the 2000 MTV Video Music Awards winning both Best Video of the Year and Best Male Video, for *The Real Slim Shady*, as well as Best

Rap Video with Dr. Dre for the track *Forgot about Dre*. At the award ceremony he took to the stage with vigorous performances of 'The Real Slim Shady' and 'The Way I Am', sending the TV network censors into an apoplectic frenzy. He also went on to win Best Album for *Marshall Mathers* and the Best Hip-Hop Artist category at the MTV Europe Awards in Stockholm.

While cementing his reputation and proving that he was no flash in the pan, one-hit wonder, there was also some good news about his turbulent relationship with Kimberley. As a result of the Hot Rocks Café incident, Kimberley had been found guilty of breach of the peace and given eleven months probation in addition to a small fine. Crucially, she was also ordered to attend Alcoholics Anonymous meetings in order to counter her growing dependence upon liquor. As she cleaned up, and the anger of the past few months receded, Eminem and Kimberley grew closer again. They were reported to be living together, and just before Christmas 2000, they both signed a formal agreement to dismiss their divorce. Kim's lawyers publicly stated that they had put their differences aside and were looking towards the future, raising Hailie Jade in a two-parent home.

Although his relationship with Kimberley now looks brighter, Eminem's relationship with his mother persists to be a constant thorn in his side. The latest development in their ongoing battle came to a head late in 2000, when she released a hip-hop single of her own. Recorded in collaboration with ID-X rapper Lamar Weeden and singer Jerome Frost, and produced by REM and Indigo Girls collaborator John Keane, 'Set The Record Straight' was intended to do just that. The lyrics of the song were an open letter in which she put forward her side of the story about his upbringing, asserting that Eminem had gone too far with his lies and that people needed to hear the truth. Apart from trying to dispel some of the myths she believes Eminem has created, she also says that she still loves him and hopes that if he ever falls she will be there to help pick up the pieces. As part of the record's promotion she even had her own website set up at *www.marshallsmom.com*, which carried streamed samples of the track, its b'sides and a gallery of photographs depicting Eminem as a child.

In a few short years, Eminem has gone from being an unknown Detroit rapper with a dream, to a multi award-winning international superstar, with record-breaking world-wide sales. It could be time for him to sit back, take stock and enjoy what he has achieved. This, however, is not for Eminem. He looks set to go from strength to strength, defying critics who say that the only direction for him now is down. But where exactly does he go from here?

In addition to working on a follow-up album to *The Marshall Mathers LP*, Eminem also looks set to move into acting. Following his cameo appearance in the low-budget, straight to video, horror spoof *The Hip-Hop Witch*, *Variety* magazine has reported that he is in negotiations with film executives to appear in the new Denzil Washington thriller *Training Day*. The movie is set to start shooting in the Spring of 2001, with *Replacement Killers* director Antoine Fuqua at the helm, and is supposed to feature Eminem as the villain. The story revolves around a Los Angeles cop, played by Washington, who is given the task of training a rookie narcotics officer. Eminem has also mentioned a possible future film project of his own that will rely heavily on biographical events from his life.

Although the well-trodden path from music to film looks like a fruitful route to follow, Eminem may very well be prevented from doing any further work at all in the near future. As a result of the two gun-related incidents, there is a real possibility that he will have to serve some time in jail. Although Eminem, surprisingly, has a previously clean criminal record, prosecutors, in both Oakland and Macomb county, have refused to accept plea bargains and are now pushing for custodial sentences. The Oakland charges, which resulted from his run-in with ICP staffer Douglas Dail, are for the relatively minor offences of brandishing a firearm and possession of a concealed weapon, and on balance it looks likely that he will only get probation if convicted. However, in Macomb County, Eminem is facing the much more serious charge of assault with a deadly weapon. The prosecutors in this case consider that the alleged pistol-whipping of John Guerra outside the Hot Rocks Café is not an offence that should be allowed to pass with just a rap on the knuckles. All the predictions are that, if convicted, Eminem will serve anything from two months to two years in jail. Once the current criminal trials are over though, Eminem still has to fight a civil lawsuit filed against him by Guerra, in which he is claiming damages of $25,000, for alleged physical assault and emotional distress.

Eminem also looks set to continue his battles with censors everywhere. He has already seriously tested the permissible borders of free speech, and it looks to be an area that he will push even further in the future. On past form, there is no doubt that he will attract an ever-increasing amount of criticism from various moral guardians, with calls for tighter regulation and even outright censorship of his music. It now looks likely that several countries will introduce a new classification scheme for recordings, which will operate along similar lines to that used for movies and legally prevent minors from purchasing adult-themed material. A scheme like this already operates in New Zealand, where the authorities gave *The Marshall Mathers LP* an R18 classification, prohibiting anyone from selling, or even giving a copy, to anyone under 18. As a result of this scheme, record shops that are found to be selling to anyone under-age could face a fine of up to $25,000. In the US, authorities have long favoured tighter self-regulation of the music industry, fearing that the 'parental advisory' warnings on the front of album covers are not enough to prevent explicit material falling into the hands of children. While the constitutional right to free-speech would certainly prevent an all out ban on Eminem's music, if current proposals for an industry regulated age classification system are unsuccessful, then there is a real chance that government-imposed legislation will follow. Whatever happens in the future though, we can be certain that the music industry's card is now well and truly marked and they are going to have to be much more careful with regards to who they sell their products to in the future.

With several pending courts cases, authorities world-wide banning him from appearing and feminist and gay groups joining the condemnation due to some of the content of his lyrics, has Eminem gone one step too far and shot himself in the foot? Quite probably not. Outrage and controversy have never done much harm to the careers of rock stars and Mr Mathers seems to be following a well-trodden path. Whatever he does and however his career develops, if anything's true of Eminem it's his unpredictability, and all we know for sure is that he's going to surprise us all again and again.

SOLO ALBUMS AND EP'S:

Infinite: *Infinite / W.E.G.O. / It's Ok / 313 / Tonite / Maxine / Open Mic / Never 2 Far / Searchin / Backstabber / Jealousy Woes II*
LP - Web Entertainment 1997 - (No longer available)

The Slim Shady EP: *Intro (Slim Shady) / Low, Down, Dirty / If I Had... / Just Don't Give A Fuck / Mommy / Just the Two Of Us / No One's Iller / Murder, Murder / If I Had (radio edit) / Just Don't Give A Fuck (radio edit)*
EP - Web Entertainment 1998 - (No longer available)

The Slim Shady LP: *Public Service Announcement Intro / My Name Is... / Guilty Conscience / Brain Damage / Paul / If I Had / 97 Bonnie and Clyde / Bitch / Role Model / Lounge / My Fault / Ken Kaniff / Cum On Everybody / Rock Bottom / Just Don't Give A Fuck / Soap / As The World Turns / I'm Shady / Bad Meets Evil / Still Don't Give A Fuck / Album Snippet Tape*
(Limited edition bonus disc also includes the tracks: *Hazardous Youth Acapella* and *Greg Acapella*)
LP - Aftermath / Interscope 1999

The Marshall Mathers LP Promo Tape: *Intro / Fatbeats / The Real Slim Shady / Curtis / Freestyle 1 / Men With Van / Marshall Mathers / Carry Out / Freestyle 2 / Rex / Criminal / Mimi*
LP - Aftermath / Interscope 2000

The Marshall Mathers LP: *Public Service Announcement 2000 / Kill You / Stan / Paul / Who Knew / Steve Berman / The Way I Am / The Real Slim Shady / Remember Me? / I'm Back / Marshall Mathers / Ken Kaniff / Drug Ballad / Amityville / Bitch Please II / Kim / Under The Influence / Criminal*
(Also available in a version with the bonus track *The Kids*).
LP - Aftermath / Interscope 2000

SOLO SINGLES:

Just Don't Give A Fuck
12-inch single - Universal/Interscope 1988

My Name Is...: *Clean version / Extra Dirty Version*
12-inch single - Interscope 1999

Guilty Conscience: *Clean w/chorus / Dirty w/chorus* (Video Mix)
12-inch promo - Interscope 1999

EMINEM PSYCHO

EMINƎM
INFINITE

EMINƎM
THE MARSHALL MATHERS LP

PARENTAL ADVISORY

EMINEM
THE SHADY MATHERS SESSIONS

EMINƎM

HEARTBREAKING WORKS OF STAGGERING GENIUS
THE SADDEST ALBUMS EVER!

NEW MUSICAL NME EXPRESS

12 AUGUST 2000 £1.15 $[US]4.75
http://www.nme.com

ECKŌ
YOU'RE NICKED!

THE FACE EM

Entered Eminem

ARE THERE NO LIMITS?

FILTH · HUMOUR · VIOLENCE & HATE
AND POP CULTURE — HAS SHOWBIZ
FINALLY GONE TOO FAR?

THE
UP IN SMOKE
TOUR
FEATURING

DRE SNOOP DOGG EMINEM ICE

PARENTAL ADVISORY
EXPLICIT CONTENT

sizzling music special!

rodney jerkins
timo maas
björk
roni size /
reprazent

5

PARENTAL ADVISORY
EXPLICIT CONTENT

EMINEM
UNAUTHORIZED AND UNCENSORED!

eminem
'I'm not scared

Eminem
SHADY HITS
BRIXTON

EMINEM
GUILTY CONSCIENCE
FEATURING DR. DRE
INCLUDES 'MY NAME IS' VIDEO CD ROM

PARENTAL ADVISORY
EXPLICIT LYRICS

THE
Slim Shady
LP

EMINEM
THE REAL SLIM SHADY

Guilty Conscience Pt 2: *Radio / Instrumental / My Name Is... /
My Name Is...* (CD Rom Video)
CD Single - Interscope 1999

The Way I Am: *Album Version / Clean Edit / Kids (Uncensored) / '97 Bonnie
and Clyde / Steve Berman / Real Slim Shady*
CD Single - Interscope 2000

The Real Slim Shady
CD Single - Polydor 2000

Stan: *Stan (Radio Edit) / Guilty Conscience (Radio Version) / Hazardous
Youth (Accapella Version) / Get You Mad*
CD Single - Interscope 2000

ALBUMS AND EPS WITH OTHER ARTISTS / SOUNDTRACKS:

Soul Intent: *F#@!in Backstabber / Biterphobia* — Soul Intent
Audio Cassette - Mashin' Deck Records 1996

Green and Gold: *Green and Gold* - The Anonymous
EP - Goodvibe Records 1998

Attack Of the Weirdos: *Trife Thieves* - Bizarre
EP - Federation 1998

Episode 1: *We Shine* - Da Ruckus
EP - Federation 1998

The Underground EP: *Bring Our Boys / Filthy / Chance to Advance* - D12
Featuring Eminem
EP - Dirty Dozen 1998

Devil Without A Cause: *Fuck Off* - Kid Rock
LP - Atlantic Records 1998

Power Cypher 3: *Freestyle* - Tony Touch
LP - Touch Ent. 1999

Behind The Doors of the 13th Floor: *Hustlers and Hardcore* - Domingo
LP - Roadrunner 1999

Tell Em Why U Madd: *Still...Crazy* - Madd Rapper featuring Eminem
LP - Columbia 2000

Skull & Bones: *Rap Superstar* - Cypress Hill featuring Eminem
LP - Sony/Columbia 2000

Game Over: *Hellbound* (H&H Remix) - Eminem, J-Black, & Masta Ace
LP - Yosumi 1999

The Nutty Professor 2 Soundtrack: *Off The Wall* - Eminem and Redman
LP - Universal/Def Jam 2000

60 Minutes of Funk Vol. 4: *Words Are Weapons* - FunkMaster Flex
featuring D12 & Eminem
LP - Loud Records 2000

Restless: *Don't Approach Me* - Xzibit featuring Eminem
LP - Loud Records 2000

SINGLES WITH OTHER ARTISTS:

5 Star Generals - Shabaam Sahdeeq featuring Eminem, Kewst, Skam and A.L.
12-inch single - Rawkus Records 1998

ThreeSixtyFive - OldWorlDisorder featuring Eminem
12-inch single - Beyond Real Recordings 1988

Bad Meets Evil: *Nuttin' To Do / Scary Movies* - Eminem & Royce
12-inch single - Beyond Real Recordings 1988

The Anthem - Sway & Tech featuring Eminem, RZA, Kool G. Rap,
Xzibit, Pharoah Monch, Tech 9ne, KRS-One, Jayo Felony
12-inch single - Interscope Records 1999

Macosa - Outsidaz featuring Eminem
12-inch single - Ruffnation 1999

Rock / Watch Dees - DJ Spinna featuring Eminem
CD Single - Rawkus 1999

Shit On You - D12 featuring Eminem
12-inch Single - Interscope/Shady Records 2000

The One - Royce Da 5'9 featuring Eminem
12-inch Single - Game Records 2000

MP3:

My Name Is… - Rock Star Remix
MP3 - Eminem.Com Exclusive 1999

Three Verses
MP3 - Eminem.Com Exclusive 1999

Pick It Up - (Live)
MP3 - Eminem.Com Exclusive 1999

Just Rhymin' With Proof - Eminem & Proof Freestyle in Paris
MP3 - Eminem.Com Exclusive 2000

UNRELEASED TRACKS:

Our House - Unreleased track from "The Marshall Mathers LP" featuring Limp Bizkit
Turn Me Loose - Unreleased track from Limp Bizkit's "Significant Other" LP featuring Eminem
Drastic Measures – Track fuelling Eminem's feud with Cage
Tylonol Island
Shroomz
Go To Hell
Hard Act To Follow
Showdown

BOOTLEGS / REMIXES AND FREESTYLES:

There are many hundreds of bootleg CDs, 12-inch White Labels and MP3s of Eminem's music. The following are a selection of the most popular remixes and freestyles as well official released and unreleased tracks.

BOOTLEGS:

Eminem – Fucking Crazy: Fucking Crazy / Forget about Dre (feat. Dr. Dre) / Anonymous (Green and Gold) / The Shutdown (Dr.Dre feat. Eminem) / Nuttin'ta do (Royce Da 5'9 feat. Eminem) / Watch Dees (DJ Spinna feat. Eminem) / 5 Verses / Scary Movies (Royce Da 5'9 feat. Eminem) / Get You Mad / Fuck Off (Kid Rock feat. Eminem) / Hustlers and Hardcore / The Wakeup Show (The Anthem inc. Eminem) / Bus A Rhyme (Missy Elliot feat. Eminem) / Flyset Material (High and Mighty feat. Eminem) / My Name Is… - Rock Star Remix / 5 Star Generals (Shabaam Sahdeeq feat. Eminem)

Green And Gold: Watch Deez (With Thirstin Howl II) / Any Man / Bad Guys Always Die / Open Mic / 3 Verses / Cali Kings Freestyle (with the Bakka Boys) / Just Don't Give a Fuck / (banx remix) / Green and Gold / Never 2 Far / 14 Freestyle 1-V

REMIXES:

No Turntables - Eminem, Nas, Mos Def, Ghetalion
It's Murda (Remix)
Big Pimpin (Remix)
Bling Bling (Remix)
Forgot About Dre (Remix)
Fuckin Crazy (Gangstarr Remix)
Just Dont Give A Fuck (Forgot About Dre Backround Beat Mix)
Just Dont Give A Fuck (Hail Mary Mix)
Just Dont Give A Fuck (Pete Rock Mix)
Just The Two Of Us (Will Smith Backround Beat Mix)
My Name Is (Hard Knock Life Remix)

FREESTYLES:

Eminem, Dilated Peoples, Aristotle
Eminem and Royce
Eminem Coca Bz.-Wake Up Show
Big Lincoln
Broke Rubber
Cage Diss
Distorted Verse on DJ Spinna's Mixx
Tony Touch Power 3 Verse
Eminem and KRS-One
Freestyle 1 from xl Show
Freestyle 2 from xl Show
Freestyle 3 from xl Show
Keepin It Raw
Armstrong Show with Interview
Pop Pills
Hand Me An Ape
Ice Grill In You
Rhymin Words
Gun In Hand
Born With Horns
Retarded Kid Named Greg